We Love You, Arthur

We Love You, Arthur

By Fiona Evans

New Writing North Drama

Published by New Writing North 2005

First published in 2005 by
New Writing North
2 School Lane
Whickham
Newcastle upon Tyne
NE16 4SL

New Writing North Limited 3166037
Registered charity number 1062729

ISBN 0-9541456-6-6

Series editor: Claire Malcolm
Typesetting and production design: John Adair
Printed by Cromwell Press

Caution
All rights whatsoever in this play are strictly reserved and applica-
tions for performances etc should be made to Fiona Evans c/o New
Writing North, 2 School Lane, Whickham, Newcastle upon Tyne,
NE16 4SL.

Supporters
New Writing North acknowledges the support of Arts Council
England's Grants for the Arts and Cultural Development Sector
Initiative funding programmes. The production is sponsored by
Project North East and supported via ESF and ERDF grants from
the European Union.

New Writing North presents

We Love You, Arthur

Written by Fiona Evans

First performed at the Assembly Rooms, Edinburgh Festival Fringe on 5 August 2005.

Cast in order of appearance

Lisa	Joanne Hickson
Julie	Ashlea Sanderson
Ray	John Carter
Dot/Ann/Yvonne	Zoe Lambert

Director	Mark Catley
Production designer	John Hudson

This script was published in time for the first performance. Please note that there may be minor differences between the performance and this text.

Cast and crew biographies

John Carter *Ray*

John trained at Bretton Hall. Theatre credits include *Animal Farm* (Northern Stage), *Bouncers* and *Two* (tours of the Middle East and India), *Run For Your Wife* (national tour), *Paradise Lost* (Powerhouse Theatre), *The Tempest* (Wakefield Opera House) and *FireRaisers* (Southwark Playhouse), which he also directed. TV and film work includes *Emmerdale*, *Byker Grove*, *EastEnders*, *Badger*, *Bull* and *Would Love To Meet* (Pinball Films). For BBC radio, *The Ice Factory, Sitting Ducks*.

Mark Catley *Director*

Mark Catley was born in Leeds and studied drama and theatre arts at Goldsmiths College, London. His directing credits include *Players* by Tajinder Hayer (West Yorkshire Playhouse), *Too Broke to Fix*, *The Game* and *Angel* (Angel Productions, as artistic director) and numerous youth theatre productions. His writing credits include *Sunbeam Terrace*, *Crap Dad* and *Scuffer* (West Yorkshire Playhouse) and *Flutterby* and *Car 5* for BBC Radio 4.

Fiona Evans *Writer*

We Love You, Arthur is Fiona's first professionally produced play. She is currently developing *Apace* for BBC Radio 4 and *The Virgin of Stratford* as part of the New Voices writing programme at Theatre Royal Stratford East. Past credits include *How to Marry a Footballer* (Challenge Theatre Company), which was the first play to be performed at The Stadium of Light, and *Whose Science is it Anyway?* by North Tyneside Youth Theatre.

Joanne Hickson *Lisa*

Joanne Hickson is a BA (Hons) Performing Arts graduate, a founder member of Live Youth Theatre and a Stagecoach Theatre School student. She has appeared in a variety of television dramas for Granada and BBC.

John Hudson *Production designer*
John trained at Central School of Speech and Drama before
working in the West End at Her Majesty's Theatre. He has worked
extensively in the North East as a freelance designer. His work as
associate designer for Live Theatre in Newcastle includes *In Blackberry
Time*, *Kidder's Luck*, *Hair in the Gate*, *Seafarers*, *Laughter When We're Dead*,
NE1, *When We Were Queens*, *Tales from the Backyard* and *Bones*.

Susie Jenkins *Stage manager*
Susie Jenkins is currently studying at Newcastle College, where she
has stage managed *Five Short Plays by Chekhov*, *Gulliver's Travels* and *The
Opening Ceremony* along with *Burn* and *Citizenship*, (Theatre Royal,
Newcastle).

Zoe Lambert *Dot / Ann / Yvonne*
Native to Yorkshire, Zoe trained in Newcastle upon Tyne. Theatre
credits include *The Bells*, *Sweet William* and *Comedy of Errors* (Northern
Broadsides); *Trouble Under Foot*, *The Terrible Grump*, *Threepenny Opera*,
Hogwash and *Out of the Blue* (Northern Stage); *As You Like It*, *Dawn of the
Firefawn* and *Tartuffe* (NTC); *Tales From the Backyard*, *Cabaret* and *Personal
Belongings* (Live Theatre); *The B.F.G.* (Bolton Octagon); *Dan Dare*,
(Customs House); *Why Do Bees Buzz?* (The Dukes); *The Millennium Show*
(Natural Theatre Company at the Millennium Dome); *The Edible City*,
(West Yorkshire Playhouse); *Tea For Two*, (Living Memory); *The Terrible
Grump*, *Feast* and *Trouble Under Foot*, (Monster Productions); and
Personal Belongings (Live Theatre) at the Edinburgh Festival 2002.
Television and film credits include: 'Rachel Whatmore' in *Emmerdale*
(Granada); *School For Seduction* (Ipso Facto); *Harry and the Hormones*
(Northmen/Different/Granada); *Waiters* (Granada/PMP); and *Byker
Grove* (BBC/Zenith). Zoe has also worked as a vocalist with the band
Friends of Harry, Briana Corrigan (ex Beautiful South) and Merz.

Ashlea Sanderson *Julie*
Ashlea graduated from Rose Bruford College in 2002. Her theatre
work includes *Missing* (Theatre Centre national tour) and *Flight Paths*
(North East tour). Her film work includes *Goal!*

CHARACTERS

Lisa Jackson
A pretty 14-year-old girl, the only daughter of Ray and Ann.

Julie Burns
Lisa's best mate.

Ray Jackson
Lisa's dad, 39.

Ann Jackson
Lisa's mam, 38.

Dot Stavers
Ann's mother, 57.

Yvonne Makepeace
The village policeman's wife.

PROLOGUE

The Big Meeting: Durham racecourse, July 1984

Ravel's Bolero *plays as the audience enters. A handmade banner, a bed sheet, is hanging from a wall. It reads: 'Coal NOT Dole – We Love You Arthur'. As the music reaches its thunderous crescendo, blackout.*

A colliery brass band plays above the sound of the crowd and children laughing. Lights up on Lisa, Julie and Ray, leaning over the wall. Lisa and Julie are sporting 1980s big hair, leggings, 'Frankie says: coal not dole' T-shirts and multiple thick layered socks which resemble leg warmers. Julie wears a pair of glasses held together with a plaster. They are singing their version of Let's Hear It For the Boy. *Ray wears a Sunderland football shirt and a child's plastic police helmet, with 'coal not dole' stickers on it. He is soaking up the atmosphere while drinking a can of beer. Lisa and Julie break off from the song, giggling with excitement.*

Lisa   I can't wait to see him, Julie.

Julie   Me too. Do you think he'll look like what he does on the telly?

Lisa   Yeah, but he'll be even better.

Julie   We'll have to get near the front, cos I won't be able to see him with these glasses, they're knackered.

Lisa   I can't wait.

Julie   What if he doesn't turn up?

Ray   He'll turn up alright lass, he's a man of his word.

Lisa   Dad! You shouldn't be listening. Will you take that hat off!

Ray   It's only a bit of fun.

Lisa   Dad!

Ray   If it makes you happy.

Ray removes the helmet.

Julie   Mr Jackson, what do you think he'll talk about?

Ray   Whey, the strike of course, yer pair of nougats.

Julie   We know that, but what's he gonna say?

Ray   I'm a miner not a bloody mind reader! And me name's RAY.

Julie   Me feet are killin'.

Ray   I'm not surprised in those shoes, they look like instruments of torture.

Julie   They're Lisa's.

Ray   Who bought you them?

Lisa   You! Before the strike. Julie man, you should have worn your Hi-Tecs or your Doc Martens.

Julie   I'm only wearing them so that I can see Arthur over the crowd.

Lisa   (*To Ray*) Do you think we'll get close enough to ask for his autograph?

Ray   What the hell do you want with his autograph?

Julie   Lisa wants his picture signing to put on her bedroom wall.

Lisa   So do you.

Ray   (*Laughing*) It's Arthur Scargill we're going to see, not George bloody Michael.

Lisa   We don't like George Michael.

Julie   He's too hairy.

Ray   I bet George has got more hair on his arse than Arthur has for a thatch.

Lisa   Don't be so disgustin'.

Julie   We're not daft kids you know, we're too old to be running around like teeny boppers, we're nearly fifteen.

Ray   With a crush on a middle-aged ginger bloke with a comby-over. (*Camping it up*) I prefer George Michael meself!

Lisa   He's not gay!

Ray   I bloody know that, only an idiot would think George was gay. I was just saying, that if I was a fourteen-year-old lass...

Julie   Mr Jackson, you're mad.

Ray   I'd be more into gorgeous George than old Shredded Wheat bonce.

Lisa   Don't let me mam hear you say that, she'll set the women's action group on you, for callin' King Arthur.

Ray   I'm only messin'. It could be worse, it could be Neil Kinnock.

Julie   I like ginger hair.

Lisa   Judas had ginger hair! Mrs Hall says so.

Ray   Well, you know what I think of Kinnock, but Arthur's nee Judas, he's more like Moses.

Lisa   Well, he's our Che Guevara.

Ray   But uglier.

Lisa   Beauty is in the eye of the beholder.

Julie   (*Whispered*) It's a good job for him, that your mam thinks so. (*Girls laugh*)

Ray   I hope you two are not taking the rise?

Lisa   As if we would.

Ray takes off his T-shirt.

Ray   By, it's a scorcher today.

Julie   Mr Jackson!

Lisa   Dad!

Ray   I'm boiling. All the lads from the village have got them off.

Lisa   And look at the state of them.

Ray   I'm in better shape now than I ever have been, look at me tan, this strike's good for something.

Lisa   You're so embarrasin'.

Julie   Your dad's crackers.

Lisa   Ha'way, let's leave him with the rest of the Village People and try to get down the front – we'll get a better view.

Ray   Is your dad not coming down, Julie?

Julie   Me mam had some jobs for him to do, he couldn't get away.

Ray   They must be important if Tommy's missing the big meeting.

Julie   I feel sorry for him, she's always on his back.

Lisa   Ha'way Julie, we'll miss 'im.

The lights fade, Arthur Scargill is speaking and the crowd is cheering. Lights up on Lisa and Julie watching Arthur, who is on stage giving a speech.

Lisa   He must be boiling up there.

Julie   Look, he's mopping his brow.

Lisa   He's so committed.

Julie   So passionate

Lisa   A right firebrand.

Julie   He's taking his jacket off.

Lisa   Look at the way he loosens his tie, the way he grips that knot firmly.

Julie   Arghh, me glasses are steaming up!

Lisa   He's one of us, Julie.

Julie   He's gonna stop her, isn't he, Lise? He's gonna stop Thatcher.

Lisa   Aye he is, how could he not, look at him, he's like a staffy in a fight, he won't let go until the bitter end.

They are listening to Arthur Scargill's speech: "Let me say one thing clearly, that miners throughout the length and breadth of the British coalfield are all going to suffer the same fate unless we stand firmly together."

Julie   Like King Arthur says, it's just a matter of stickin' together.

Lisa   Together forever.

Julie   Together forever.

Julie and Lisa   We love you, Arthur!

Sound of the crowd cheering. Blackout.

SCENE ONE

Dot's living room, October 1984

Dot is watching the final scene of Casablanca; *in her mind she is on the runway with Rick and Ilsa, mouthing the words which she knows off by heart, she has tears in her eyes. A book, Oscar Wilde's* Soul of Man Under Socialism *is open, face down on the floor. Ray sits nearby. He is reading the* Daily Mirror.

Dot   "If that plane leaves the ground and you're not with him, you'll regret it. Maybe not today, maybe not tomorrow, but soon and for the rest of your life."

Ray   Do we have to have a running commentary?

Dot   Shush man! This is me favourite bit.

Lisa and Julie enter. Lisa is carrying a plastic bag of dirty washing. They have seen her watching this film a million times.

Ray   (*Puts his finger to his mouth and points to the TV*) Shush.

Dot   "But it doesn't take much to work out that the problems of three little people don't amount to a hill of beans in this crazy world." Sorry lasses, I haven't seen Humphrey say that in a while.

Ray   It must be at least two days.

Lisa picks up the book from the floor.

Lisa   Oscar Wilde?

Dot   Soul of man under Socialism.

Ray   Your nana's not just a pretty face.

Lisa   Morrissey likes Oscar Wilde

Julie   Your nana's dead 'with it'.

Julie snatches the book off her, reads a bit, looks perplexed, then hands it back.

Dot   Who's Morrissey?

Lisa   Just the greatest singer in the best band in the whole world?

Ray   (*Winding them up*) He didn't sing with the Rolling Stones.

Julie   The Smiths!

Lisa   Heaven knows I'm miserable now!

Dot   You're such a drama queen.

Ray   (*To Dot*) I don't know who she gets it from.

Julie   It's a Smiths song. (*Sings*) "I was looking for a job and then I found a job, and heaven knows I'm miserable now."

Dot   Urrh, not that miserable racket, it was on the wireless earlier on.

Lisa   Nana, it's full of lyrical humour.

Ray   It bloody made me laugh. Why's he so miserable, eh? When he's just found a job? Half the blokes round here would be over the moon with a new job. (*Lisa and Julie look at each other, shaking their heads in disbelief at how he doesn't appreciate Morrissey's obvious genius*)

Dot   So, this Morrissey bloke has made Oscar fashionable, has he? He must have good taste.

Ray   Do you think he'd approve of your crush on Arthur Scargill!

Lisa   It's Julie who fancies Arthur. I'm more interested in his mind.

Julie   Eee, you little liar.

Dot   Never be ashamed of your feelings, pet, or your beliefs – sometimes it's the only thing you can trust. I'm only kiddin', Arthur's better looking in real life, always immaculately turned out. The television doesn't do him justice.

Ray   Your nana's met him.

Lisa and Julie   You've met him!

Dot   Only for a minute.

Lisa   When?

Dot   We'd raised some money for some fund, we were handing over the cheque. I've got the photo somewhere.

Julie   What did he smell like?

Dot   He smelt of Old Spice aftershave

Ray   And hairspray.

Julie   Hairspray?

A dog starts whining.

Dot   The dog needs walking. The lead's in the cupboard.

Ray   Don't let the bugger off or she'll be away. I'm sure she's coming into heat.

Dot   Maggie, go for walkies!

Julie laughs.

Dot   What's so funny?

Julie   You calling your dog Maggie.

Dot   Lisa's grandad wanted to call her Arthur. I said you cannot call her a lad's name.

Lisa   I'm surprised grandad let you call her Maggie though. (*To Julie*) He hated Thatcher.

Dot   Well, when she was a pup, she was the bossy one in the litter, always stealing the milk off the other pups; ginger and a milk snatcher – what else could we call her?

Julie   Arthur's our favourite name.

Ray   Every ginger staffy in the colliery is called Arthur. Even the polis round the corner has got one called Scargill.

The dog whines.

(To Lisa and Julie) Are you taking that dog out?

Lisa   In a minute.

Dot   What's in the bag?

Lisa   Me mam's sent some washing round, the machine's knackered.

Ray   Again?

Dot   Could she not bring it up herself?

Lisa   She's working up the soup kitchen.

Dot   She seems to be spending a lot of time up there, *(To Ray)* I see more of you than I do of her.

Ray   Lucky lady.

Lisa   We won't be long.

Ray   I'm away too, I've got to feed the pigeons. *(To Lisa)* Remember, don't let her off the lead.

Ray exits.

Julie   *(Impersonating Barbara Woodhouse)* Walkies!

Lisa and Julie leave. Dot starts sorting through the washing bag. She takes out a pair of man's jeans. She is automatically searching through all the pockets. She pulls out a very saucy birthday card. She is momentarily confused. She opens it and reads. She can't quite believe what she is reading. She slowly folds it back up and puts it in her handbag.

SCENE TWO

Walking the dog

The back field. Lisa is holding the lead. Every now and then the dog pulls her.

Julie I can't believe your nana's met him, Lisa.

Lisa And me mam didn't even tell us.

Julie Maybe she didn't know?

Lisa Ha'way man, Julie, how could she not know?

Julie Well, they don't get on.

Lisa Me dad gets on better with me nana, he's more outgoing, she's too shy.

Julie Your mam's not shy, she's always out doing strike stuff and collecting money.

Lisa She never used to be. Six months ago, she wouldn't have said boo to a goose, never mind knocking on people's doors.

Julie Oh my god, that's it!

Lisa What yer talkin' about, you loony!

Julie Collecting money! If we raise enough money for the strike fund, then we might get to hand the cheque over to Arthur, like your nana did.

Lisa You're a genius, Julie, a bloody genius!

Julie Am I?

Lisa   Yes. But if we're gonna get to meet him, we'll have to keep the money separate, to prove we've raised it. We can't just collect with the others.

Julie   OK.

Lisa   We've got to come up with a good idea.

Julie   (*Thinking*) We could do a sponsored silence.

Lisa   You?

Julie nods, keeping her lips firmly shut to demonstrate her ability.

Lisa   You'd never be able to do it.

Julie   Yes, I would.

Lisa   See.

Julie   Arrh! You tricked us.

Lisa   Maybe we could have a bring 'n' buy sale?

Julie   Who's gonna buy?

Lisa   Yeah, everyone's skint.

Julie   We could collect stuff, milk bottle tops, or stamps.

Lisa   Where would we take them?

Julie   Write to *Blue Peter*, they'll know.

Lisa   They only get money cos they've got millions of kids collecting them, we're never gonna make anything with just us two.

Long pause.

Julie   Maybe we could go busking.

Lisa   We haven't got any instruments and we can't sing.

Julie   I've got me recorder.

Lisa   You can only play one tune.

Julie   It might go down well, a whole afternoon of *London's Burning* in Durham marketplace.

Lisa   You'd get stoned!

Julie   I could learn some Smiths.

Lisa   How long would that take?

Julie   Ages.

Lisa   And everyone from school would see us.

Julie   I'm not bothered. If we get to meet Arthur, I'd strip naked and run over Elvet Bridge.

Lisa   I suppose so.

Julie   There's nee supposing about it.

The dog yanks the lead.

Julie   How does your nana manage her?

Lisa   She doesn't. Me nana doesn't like leaving the house, she's got that agoraphobia. Me dad takes her out for walks.

Julie   Your dad's great.

Lisa   (*Embarrassed*) Julie!

Julie   Well he is, not like mine. He doesn't even go picketing.

Lisa   Why not?

Julie   Me mam won't let him.

Lisa   But he could get two quid a day for it.

Julie   She doesn't care.

Lisa   Really? Even my mam's been on the picket line, but me da said she should stay away, it's too dangerous for women.

Julie   I'd love a mam and dad like yours.

Lisa   You can have them.

Julie   Maybe I should put meself up for adoption.

Lisa   What if you ended up with someone worse than your mam and dad?

Julie   Worse?

Lisa   Like the copper and his wife, then I wouldn't be able to talk to you – it'd be like you being a scab.

Julie   Lisa!

Lisa   Well, you could end up with them, they haven't got kids. Me dad reckons PC plod fires blanks. He gets some right stick on the picket line.

Julie   Eee, that's awful, I don't suppose test-tube babies had been invented back then.

Lisa   The first one, Louise Brown, was born in 1978, I read it in me midwife book.

Julie She had a funny shaped head.

Lisa She didn't.

Julie She did, it must have been from being (*She flattens her hands against her cheeks to create an elongated face*) up against the glass. (*They laugh*)

Lisa She didn't grow in the test tube, they transplant them into their mother's womb.

Julie Urrh! (*Pause*) You're dead clever you, you're like your nana.

Lisa Me nana tells us lots of stuff, but if I'm really interested I'll read about it, like midwifery.

Julie Why is it that some people can't have kids, is it passed down from their parents?

Lisa laughs.

Julie What? Maybe it's not *his* fault, maybe it's *hers*? I mean, she does wear those really tight skirts. I don't know how she manages to walk the dog in those stilettos. She'd have a right time being pregnant in those heels.

Lisa She could always get someone else to have it for her.

Julie Like one of those suffragette mothers.

Lisa It's surrogate, man! The suffragettes tied themselves to the King's racehorses.

Julie I thought they tied themselves to railings.

Lisa   What would you know, you and your suffragette mothers?

Julie   It was a mistake! Anyway, I don't know how those wives can sell their babies.

Lisa   I know, I mean my nana wouldn't even part with Maggie. Mind, I think she'd have sold me mother for a few quid! Bloody hell, that's it!

Julie   What?

Lisa   Selling babies, making some money, to meet Arthur.

Julie   You mean kidnap?

Lisa   Not quite.

Julie   Where we gonna get them from?

Lisa   Make them!

Julie   I'm not 'doing it' with anyone.

Lisa   Not us.

Julie   Well who then?

The dog tugs at the lead, Lisa nods towards the dog.

Lisa   Good girl Maggie, you know what I'm talking about, you're gonna help us meet Arthur.

Julie   Hang on, you're saying that we get the dog pregnant, and then we get to meet Arthur.

Lisa   Yes.

Julie   How does that work?

Lisa   Surely I don't have to draw you diagrams.

Julie   Not about that. How do we go from having a load of puppies, to getting to meet Arthur?

Lisa   They are worth a fortune, you can get hundreds of pounds for one pedigree pup.

Julie   Brilliant! That's a great idea. Hang on a minute, who are we gonna sell them to? Everyone's skint around here.

Lisa   We'll put an advert in the paper.

Julie   You need money for that.

Lisa   Well, in a shop then, where people have got money, somewhere posh.

Julie   Like Sunderland.

Lisa   Sunderland?

Julie   My auntie's best friend's sister lives in Ashbrooke, in Sunderland. And they're dead posh. They've got two bathrooms in one house and a whirlpool bath.

Lisa   Wow! A whirlpool bath? Ashbrooke it is, we'll sell our puppies in Ashbrooke.

Julie   Don't get too excited, we haven't got a dad yet, and the puppies are only worth a fortune if they're pedigrees. Where are we gonna get a proper pedigree staffy from?

Lisa   (*Does bad impersonation of a police officer*) Hello hello hello.

Julie   (*Giggling*) Hello.

Lisa You're nicked! (*Julie looks amused, but says nothing*) I'm talking about Scargill, the copper's dog. He's gonna be the puppies' dad.

Julie The copper will never agree to that, he'd want some of the money.

Lisa That's why we're gonna keep this to ourselves.

Julie Just take the copper's dog? That's kidnap! What if we get arrested?

Lisa It's not kidnap. It's dognap. They'd never arrest us for that.

Julie Will there be a ransom?

Lisa We're not holding him hostage, we'll just borrow him for a while.

Julie What if your nana finds out?

Lisa She's gonna find out eventually. Do you want to meet Arthur or not?

Julie Course I do.

Lisa Well then, we've got to plan this carefully, like what the pickets do with the police. Like a military operation.

Julie Maybe we should give it a name.

Lisa Yes. Operation...

Julie Ginger Comby-over.

Lisa Phase one.

SCENE THREE

Plans interrupted

Lisa's bedroom. Operation Ginger Comby-over outfits are laid out on the bed. Lisa has a clipboard and pen.

Lisa　Two black T-shirts?

Julie　Check.

Lisa　Two black socks?

Julie　Check. Well, there's four.

Lisa　I meant pairs.

Julie　Check.

Lisa　Two pairs of black gloves.

Julie　Fingerless, like Madonna.

Julie tries them on, modelling them in front of Lisa.

Julie　(*Singing*) Like a virgin, Ooh...

Lisa　Was that a check?

Julie　Check. Do you like Madonna?

Lisa　(*Disappointed in her*) Madonna?

Julie　Neither do I. I like the Smiths.

Lisa　Julie, we are going to have to concentrate, if Operation Ginger Comby-over is going to be a success.

Julie   I know. Two pairs of black fingerless gloves, *not* like Madonna's, check. Give us that list.

Lisa   Julie, that's my job.

Julie   (*Reading*) Two balaclavas?

Lisa   I couldn't get them.

Julie   Thank god, we'd look like the Milk Tray man. I couldn't wear one anyway, I'm claustrophobic.

Lisa   I'd decided against balaclavas, they might draw unwanted attention, that's why I've got these.

Lisa produces two customised flat caps with badges and hand-produced DayGlo 'We Love you Arthur' stickers on.

Julie   Wow!

Lisa   There was an article in *Just Seventeen* about how to customise your jeans, so I took the idea and nicked me dad's cap.

Julie   Where did you get the other one?

Lisa   It's me grandad's old one.

Julie   Can I wear your dad's?

Lisa   They're both the same.

Julie looks pleadingly at her.

Lisa   If it makes you happy.

Julie sniffs it.

Lisa   Julie!

Julie tries it on.

Julie   How do I look?

Ann   (*Voice off stage*) Lisa!

Lisa   Shit, it's me mam. Hide all this stuff.

They frantically hide things and then pretend to look relaxed. Ann enters, carrying some freshly ironed washing.

Julie   Hello, Mrs Jackson.

Ann   Hello pet, what are you two up to then?

Julie   Nothing!

Lisa   Just reading some magazines.

Julie   Do you like Madonna, Mrs Jackson?

Ann   Madonna?

Lisa   The one you didn't like on *Top of the Pops*.

Ann   Her that sings that *Like a* (quietly) *Virgin*. No, I don't like her, Julie.

Julie   Neither do we, we like The Smiths.

Lisa   And Billy Bragg.

Ann   He's lovely, that Billy Bragg. Jude from the women's action group said he did a benefit gig for the miners at that place in Sunderland, erm... The Bunker.

Julie   Yeah, Madonna's rubbish.

Ann   Don't get me started on her. As Jude said, the suffragettes didn't go chaining themselves to railings to get women
the vote, just to have it all ruined by Madonna flashing her
bra off to the world.

Julie   See, I told you the suffragettes tied themselves to
railings.

Ann   Did you know that one of them, a Geordie, threw
herself under the King's racehorse at the Derby.

Lisa   Typical Geordies, always showing off.

Julie   You said it was the Grand National!

Lisa   Well, I knew it had something to do with racehorses.

Julie   Aye, but they didn't tie themselves to the saddles.

Ann   No need to be fighting amongst ourselves.

Lisa   (*Mimicking Ann*) Jude said we shouldn't be fighting
amongst ourselves.

Ann   There's no need to be like that, Lisa.

Julie   She's only funning, Mrs Jackson.

Ann   I better be off up the kitchen, we're expecting a
delivery from Russia.

Julie   Russia?

Ann   Yes, the Russian miners are sending over a lorry load
of food.

Julie   From Russia with Love.

Lisa   Not those meatballs again.

Ann   You should be grateful.

Julie   I like meatballs.

Ann   So do I, pet, but to tell you the truth, we can't read what's on the tins. We don't know whether we are gonna get meatballs or prunes.

Ray enters.

Ray   (*To Ann*) Have you seen me cap?

Ann   How should I know where it is?

Julie   Hello, Mr Jackson.

Ray   Are you round here again? I think we should change your name by deed poll, from Burns to Jackson and then we could claim some child benefit for you.

Lisa   Mam, you'll be late, for Jude.

Ann   I hardly get a chance to see you these days.

Lisa   That's what me nana said.

Ray   I know the feeling.

Ann   (*To Ray*) A bit of support would be nice. (*To Lisa*) Has she been moaning on to you again?

Lisa   No. You'll be late.

Julie   For your international date.

Ann   Tara pet. (*Kisses Lisa*) Bye Julie.

Julie   Bye, Mrs Jackson.

Ray   Come here, gorgeous. (*He grabs Ann, pretending to snog her. Julie looks bemused*)

Lisa   Urrhh.

Ann   You daft bugger. Tara.

Ann exits.

Lisa   (*Mimicking Julie*) Bye, Mrs Jackson. I like meatballs.

Julie   I'm interested!

Ray   Have you seen me cap anywhere?

Lisa   No.

Julie   Do you like Madonna, Mr Jackson?

Lisa   Not again.

Ray   She's bloody lovely. What man wouldn't?

Lisa   Dad!

Ray   I'm not drawing me pension yet. Mind, if Thatcher has her way, it might be sooner than we think.

Julie   But the miners are gonna win?

Ray   Aye pet, we are, but it's not helping matters with all these bloody scabs going back to work. I better be away, otherwise they'll be waltzing through the pit gate with no bugger to stop them.

Lisa   Go then!

Ray It's freezing out there. I'm doing the night shift. I'll need me cap.

Lisa I'm sure I saw it downstairs.

Ray Isn't that it?

Julie No, I don't...

Lisa Me mam must have brought it up with the washing.

Ray Great (*He puts it on, not noticing the stickers*) See you later, lasses. (*Doing a Wolfie Smith impersonation*) Power to the people!

Julie Bye, Mr Jackson.

Lisa Bye.

They laugh.

SCENE FOUR

Operation Ginger Comby-over

The back yard. Lisa and Julie are looking through binoculars over the yard wall.

Julie God, you can see everything with these.

Lisa Can you see the polis's dog?

Julie Not yet.

Lisa I just hope people don't think we're twitchers!

Julie Yer what?

Lisa   Twitchers, bird spotters!

Julie   They might. I can see right into the polis's wife's bedroom.

Lisa   Yer jokin'!

Julie   And I'd guess, judging by the bra hanging on the back of her chair, that she's definitely from the tit family.

They laugh.

Lisa   Gis a look.

Julie   I thought you were looking at the staffy book.

Lisa   I am.

Julie   Well, read then!

Lisa clears her throat.

Lisa   (*Reads*) "When you arrive at the stage when you wish to choose a mate for your bitch, you will need to do some careful thinking."

Julie   She's takin' him for a walk.

Lisa   You are aware that she is a pretty fair specimen...

Julie   She isn't! She's a right tart, and she's got those American tan tights on again.

Lisa   I'm on about Maggie the dog, yer idiot! "Her breeding is such" - I'm talkin' about Maggie - "that she might reasonably produce, when mated to the right dog" - that'll be Scargill - "something really good."

Julie   He's a beauty.

Lisa   Gis the binocs, it's your turn to read.

Julie   (*Scanning the page for the right place*) Da, dada, dada...
"Breeding your bitch... you may consider him a good mate for
her, but you want to be sure. He has to have a great head and
skull."

Lisa   Yes he has, very strong.

Julie   "His body is powerfully constructed."

Lisa   It is.

Julie   "... he has the right breed temperament but his ears
are just that bit untidy."

Lisa   No he's perfect.

Julie   Just like the real Scargill.

Julie and Lisa   We need that dog.

SCENE FIVE

Dognapping

*Lights up on the back lane, behind the policeman's house. Lisa and Julie both
have their 'Operation Ginger Comby-over' outfits on. Julie is struggling with
Lisa on her shoulders. We can hear an excited dog.*

Lisa   Shush Scargill.

Julie   Give him the meatballs.

Lisa   I'm trying.

Julie   Hurry up and get over, me shoulders are killin'.

A light is switched on in the policeman's house.

Lisa   Shit!

Julie   I thought they went out on a Thursday.

Lisa   The wife does. She's still in, she's coming.

Julie   Get down!

They collapse to the floor, hiding.

Yvonne (*Voice off stage*) Ha'way Scargill pet, get inside. I haven't got all night, I'll be late. Scargill! Well if you don't get in now you'll be out until that bugger comes off his shift. Bloody dog, ignoring us, you're just like that stubborn get.

Lisa   That was close.

Julie   It's a good job she was meeting someone.

Lisa   I can smell her perfume from here.

Julie   I bet she's got a bloke.

Lisa   Do you think so?

Julie   He must be desperate, I'd rather kiss the dog! Ha'way, let's get on with it before he comes back from his shift. I'll give you a leg up.

Lisa   I don't see why it's me that has to do all the hard work.

Julie   I'm giving you a leg up, aren't I? Besides, you're skinnier than me. Ready? One, two, three.

SCENE SIX

Love on the allotment

Lights up on Lisa and Julie on Ray's allotment. Pigeons are cooing. A dog growls.

Lisa   Now, Maggie, you'd better not bite Scargill. We'll be in for it if there's any permanent scarring.

Julie   Your dad's allotment is massive.

Lisa   Keep the torch pointing down, we don't want to attract attention.

Julie   No one's ganna see us up here.

Lisa   They might think we're trying to steal the vegetables, or knobble the pigeons.

Julie   Knobble the pigeons?

Lisa   Some of these pigeons are prize-winning champions. They're worth a fortune.

Julie   Then why are we going to all the trouble of mating the dogs on the off chance that Maggie might have pups? When we could have just nicked a pigeon.

Lisa   And who would we have sold it to? Besides we cannot nick off other miners.

Julie   I suppose not.

Lisa   You'd better not be getting cold feet.

Julie   Cold feet? We've just kidnapped the local copper's prize Staffordshire bull terrier.

Lisa   Alright, alright. Calm down. If we're nervous, it's gonna rub off on the dogs.

Julie   Did you get the tape recorder?

Lisa   It's behind the feed bins. But I don't think we should listen to music while they're doin' it, it might put them off.

Julie   It's not for *us*, it's for *them*.

Julie is rummaging behind the feed bins. She finds the recorder. She takes a cassette out of her pocket, loads the tape recorder and presses play. A crackly recording of Serge Gainsbourg's Je T'Aime *blares out.*

Lisa   Turn it down, you'll wake the whole bloody colliery. What's this rubbish?

Julie   Shush! Listen. It'll get them in the mood. It always does with me mam and dad.

Lisa   Ah nat! Have you heard your mam and dad doing it?

Julie   Aye, to this.

Lisa   Oh my god.

Julie   Have you not heard yours, like?

Lisa   No! It's disgusting! Me dad's nearly forty, man!

Julie   Well, maybe you should take the tape home with you? This song definitely gets them going, and I thought it might work with Maggie and Scargill.

Lisa   I'm not sure.

Julie   Even staffies have feelings. It's worth a try.

Lisa   (*Reluctantly*) Alright, we'll give it a go.

They sit looking at the dogs for a long time as the music plays.

Lisa   Do you think he could be gay?

Julie   There's no way Scargill's a puff!

Lisa   You're not supposed to say that now.

Julie   What?

Lisa   Puff.

Julie   Well, you've just said it.

Lisa   Only cos I had to let you know what the word was. It's an insult.

Julie   My dad always says it.

Lisa   Me mam goes off it, if I say owt like that about the gays. I mean loads of them are supporting the miners. We should stick together.

Julie   I suppose so. It's like Dogtanian: all for one, and one for all.

Lisa   That Jude, the one with the funny trousers. Well, she's giving me mam loads of women's books to read.

Julie   What the (*quietly*) lezza?

Lisa   Lesbian!

Julie   Sorry! It takes a while to get used to it. The lesbian.

Lisa   Anyway, she's not a lesbian. She just looks like one.

Julie   I hate all that tie-dye.

Lisa   All those Greenham Common lot wear it.

Julie   I wonder why?

Lisa   Me dad says it's to hide the muck.

Julie laughs.

Lisa   He only says it to wind me mam up. He doesn't mean it. (*Looking at the dogs*) Scargill's not interested in her, do you think he might be gay?

Julie   You can't get gay dogs!

Lisa   Whey aye, you can. Have a look in that book.

Julie   You look.

Lisa   It's that music putting them off.

Julie   How can it put them off? They reckon they were really doing it when they made this record.

Lisa   I feel sick.

Julie   Now that will put them off. I thought you wanted to be a midwife!

Lisa   Aye, I still do, but I don't have to be there at the conception. Listen to this man. "If the dog you use is an experienced one it is unlikely you will need to be there..."

Julie   Do you reckon he's... (*singing*) "Like a virgin, ooh, touched for the very first time"?

Lisa   "If he is untried at stud, then, odd though it may seem, he may not be sure at which end to start and you will need to position him at times."

Julie   I'm not gannin' anywhere near him. Don't shine the torch on him, it might put him off.

Lisa   Shush man. Look, something's happening.

Julie   Oh my God!

Lisa   It's horrible!

Julie   It looks like me mother's lipstick!

Lisa   I think he's gonna find the right end.

Julie   Go on, my son.

Lisa   Good boy Scargill, get on top.

Julie   Go on son, give Maggie a good seeing to.

They fall about laughing.

SCENE SEVEN

Dirty dogs

Lisa   Do you think we've left them long enough?

Julie   No, the book says half an hour. She'll never be pregnant yet.

Muffled adult giggling is heard off stage.   •

Julie   Shit, who's that?

Lisa   Bloody hell, they're coming this way. Quick, hide.

Lisa and Julie hide and listen to the voices off stage.

Yvonne (*Giggling*) I think I've had too much to drink.

Ray   (*Saucily*) Yvonne, my pet, I don't think I've had enough! Well not yet anyway, bonny lass. Come here.

Yvonne I've worn me stockings tonight.

Ray   I cannot see a thing. I'll just have to feel me way.

Yvonne You naughty boy!

Ray   I've been waiting for this all day. I saw him on the picket line, he doesn't know what he's missing.

Yvonne Let's not talk about that bastard – he can stuff his truncheon up his...

Ray   Shush, give us a kiss.

As they are kissing and giggling, the dogs start to bark furiously.

Yvonne Arrghh!

Ray   Jesus Christ, what the hell's going on?!

Yvonne It's our Scargill.

Ray   Get off, you little bastard! Arrhh!

A dog yelps.

Yvonne Down boy! You'll ladder me stockings.

Ray   Your stockings? He's bit me bloody arse!

Yvonne You must have scared him.

Ray There's two of the buggers! I'm starting to feel like Barbara friggin' Woodhouse.

Yvonne Ray, I better get our Scargill home. Terry'll go mad that he's escaped from the yard.

Ray (*Shouting after her*) Hang on, we haven't even, are we not ganna...? Forget it. Maggie? Is that you? What the bloody hell? Come on, I'd better get you home, Dot'll be wondering where you are.

Julie Are you alright, Lise?

Lisa He's ruined everything.

Julie It might not be what you think.

Lisa Come off it, Julie, you heard them. He was all over her.

Julie I suppose so.

Lisa She's a bloody pig's wife! He's having it off with a bloody pig's wife!

Julie I'm sorry, Lise.

Lisa I hate him.

Julie You don't mean that.

Lisa I do. Our plans are finished. There's no way Maggie's pregnant and we're never gonna meet Arthur. And it's all his fault.

Julie Are you gonna tell your mam?

Lisa   She deserves to know. She's slogging her guts out for that bastard and look what he's up to.

Julie   At least he's not back at work.

Lisa   I wish he was, at least he wouldn't have spoilt every-thing.

Julie   You don't mean that, Lisa.

Lisa   Don't I?

Julie   I'll always be here for you, you can trust me.

Lisa   That's what I thought about me dad.

SCENE EIGHT

Arthur Scargill, the lesbian

The Jacksons' living room, three weeks later.

Ray   They've asked you to do a speech?

Ann   They've not set a date, they've just asked me if I'd be interested. Why are you laughing?

Ray   I'm not. I'm pleased for you. It's just... Well, I didn't think that was your type of thing.

Ann   All of this wasn't my type of thing. Up the soup kitchen with the lasses, having a laugh. I'd never have thought I'd fit in with them, but they're great, everyone is just mucking in.

Ray   So you're having a laugh then?

Ann   It's either laugh, or cry.

Ray   Fair enough doing dishes, but a speech, you giving a speech?

Ann   You don't think I can do it?

Ray   I never said that.

Ann   You didn't have to, it's written all over your face.

Ray   Well, there must be loads of them posh birds who help out at the kitchen who've done this sort of thing before.

Ann   They want a miner's wife to do it. I just want to try something different. Surely you can understand that, Ray?

Ray   Where's our Lisa?

Ann   With Julie. She's been in a funny mood for weeks.

Ray   Well, don't look at me.

Ann   I haven't seen her properly for ages. Maybe I am spending too much time up the kitchen?

Ray   Hallelujah! And it's not gonna help matters if you're gonna be traipsing up and down the country, giving speeches with a bunch of bloody lesbians.

Ann   Just because they're feminists it doesn't mean they're lesbians. But so what if they are? To tell you the truth, I prefer their company at the minute.

Ray   You'll be burning your bloody bra next. (*More light hearted*) Or throwing yourself under the Derby winner. (*Ann does not respond*) Ha'way man, I'm only joking.

Ann   That's your excuse for everything: "I was only joking." Well, I don't need a third rate comedian, I need a husband that's going to support me, like I do him. And to put the record straight, I was actually asked to speak by the NUM. The last time I checked, Arthur Scargill wasn't a bloody lesbian.

SCENE NINE

Careless Whisper

Lisa is in her bedroom listening to George Michael's Careless Whisper. *She has a magazine on her lap. Ray enters, he is feeling awkward.*

Ray   Alright. (*Long pause*) I just thought I'd come to check that you were alright. (*Pause*) You haven't been yourself lately. There's nowt wrong, is there?

Lisa   I'd be fine if everyone stopped bothering us.

Long pause.

Lisa   What'ya staring at?

Ray   Nowt. (*Pause*) I'm sorry, I'm just, I thought you didn't like George Michael? That's why you're depressed, listening to this. (*Making fun of George singing*) "Oh, I'm never gonna dance again..."

Lisa   Do you not know the next line?

Ray   No, go on tell us.

Pause.

Lisa   It doesn't matter.

Ray   At least you're talking to us now, I was getting worried.

Lisa   I'm trying to read me magazine.

Ray   If you want to listen to some real music, I'll lend you some of me Rolling Stones.

Lisa   No thanks.

Ray   You know, if there's anything wrong, you can always talk to me.

Lisa   I'm fine.

Ray   I know pet, you're a tough un aren't you, just like your mam. And I know she's always up the soup kitchen, mebbes that's the problem?

Lisa   It's got nowt to do with me mam. Will you just get lost an leave us alone.

Ray   Alright! I'm going. I'm going.

Lisa carries on reading. Ray leaves, dejected.

SCENE TEN

Dot's advice

Dot's front room. Dot and Lisa are sitting.

Dot   Your dad should have been here hours ago. He knows I can't leave the house.

Lisa   Julie's gone for it now.

Dot   Well I hope she's quick on her pins, the post office closes at five. Your dad's gonna get it, he's a bloody law unto himself these days. (*Dot picks up the* Daily Mirror, *thinking she has said too much*) The way this lot portray the miners, it's a bloody disgrace.

Lisa   Me mam won't have it in the house.

Dot   Since when has your mother started wearing the trousers in your house?

Lisa   You want to hear her these days, she's like that Germaine Greer. Me dad doesn't know what's hit him.

Dot   She should keep him on his toes. (*Lisa looks surprised*) And she's right, why pay good money to read a pack of lies written about you? I could understand it of Murdoch's lot, but these are supposed to be left wing. It's a betrayal, that's what it is.

Lisa   Betrayal, yes it is. (*Pause*) Nana?

Dot   Yes, love.

Lisa   If you knew someone, someone who was married, was seeing someone else, would you tell on them?

Dot   Bloody hell, Lisa, where did you get that from?

Lisa   Just some lass at school was asking. Would you tell?

Dot   Well, it would depend on circumstances.

Lisa   What circumstances?

Dot   Well, things can get complicated when it comes to affairs. Well, it's true love, especially at times like these. It's like in *Casablanca* when Humphrey Bogart ends the affair with

Ingrid Bergman and he says, "The problems of three little people ain't worth a hill of beans in this crazy world." You see, they were fighting the Nazis and Humphrey knew that when you're up against something as big as fascism, your personal needs shouldn't come into it. People get hurt. What if the other person doesn't want to know?

Lisa   Surely everyone wants to know the truth.

Dot   Not always, pet, not always.

Lisa   Course they do.

Dot   Sometimes people are best left in the dark. What they don't know doesn't harm them.

Lisa   Who would want their bloke parading around behind their back with another woman?

Dot   It isn't as simple as that, love.

Lisa   What would you know?

Dot   A lot more than you think. I've been married, remember.

Lisa   Yes, but me grandad didn't cheat on you.

Dot   No, he didn't.

Lisa   Vows are supposed to be for life, not until you're bored and something better comes along.

Dot   Marriage can be boring, pet. The excitement wears off, then it's a lot of hard work.

Lisa   Well, they should work harder, especially if they've got a kid.

Dot   You're right, pet.

Lisa   I'm gonna tell her.

Dot   Tell who? (*Lisa storms out. Dot shouts after her*) Don't do anything too hasty.

Ray enters.

Ray   Is she in a mood again?

Dot   Where've you been?

Ray   Hello Ray, how are you? Lovely to see you. The weather's nice.

Dot   You were supposed to be getting me money.

Ray   I'm sorry, something cropped up.

Dot   Something or somebody?

Ray   Well, somebody, as it happens. Davy Turner. He was a man short on the picket.

Dot   And this Davy Turner, does he wear scarlet lipstick and expensive perfume?

Ray   What you talkin' about, woman?

Dot shows him the card.

Dot   No more lies, Ray.

He looks at the card in disbelief. Julie enters without being seen. She takes in the scene.

Ray   Where'd you get that from?

Dot   When I was doing the washing. It was in your jeans.

Ray   I can explain.

Dot   Really?

Ray   It was the lads mucking about.

Dot   Come off it, Ray. Of all the excuses.

Ray   You know all about excuses, you weren't exactly snow white yourself.

Dot   No, I bloody wasn't, and look what happened to me, eh, look at us. I'm stuck in this place, I'm a nervous bloody wreck, and me own daughter can't bring herself to speak to us properly after twenty years. Why do you think I'm saying this to you? Ann would never forgive you and I don't want our Lisa hurt. I don't want you to lose everything, Ray.

Ray   I'm not gonna lose anything.

Dot   I think Lisa knows.

Ray   Lisa?

Dot   She was asking strange questions.

Ray   She's fifteen, she knows nowt, cos there's nowt to know, OK? You'd better keep your mouth shut about this, you depend on me for walking that friggin' mutt and running errands. Ann will never believe anything you say.

Dot   Don't worry, Ray, I'll keep this quiet. But you can be sure it'll not be for your sake.

Ray sees Julie standing there.

Ray   Julie?

Julie   (*Nervously*) Mr Jackson.

Ray   How long have you been there?

Julie   Just got back.

Dot   She's been to get me money, because you were too busy.

Julie   Sorry Mrs Stavers, there was a queue at the post office.

Ray   You're a good lass, Julie. Don't you go changing.

SCENE ELEVEN

The speech

The Jacksons' living room moments later. Ann is reading a book. Lisa enters.

Lisa   Is the TV broke?

Ann   No, I just wanted to read.

Lisa   Mam, I need to talk to you.

Ann   After you hear me important news.

Lisa   Why are you smiling like that, you look weird?

Ann   You're not going to believe this.

Lisa   Tell us then.

Ann   It's to do with the women's group.

Lisa   Not that toy and turkey appeal?

Ann   No, not that.

Lisa   What then?

Ann   You know the rally in London, in the new year?

Lisa   The one that Arthur's gonna be at?

Ann   They've asked me to speak at it, on behalf of the miners' wives, on the stage.

Lisa   They've asked you!

Ann   Don't sound so surprised.

Lisa   You'll be on the stage with Arthur?

Ann   I suppose so. Lisa, I need you there with me. I can't do it by meself.

Lisa   With Arthur bloody Scargill!

Ann   Will you watch your language.

Lisa   Arthur Scargill. We're gonna get to meet him after all.

Ann   Yes. You are. What was it you had to tell me?

Lisa   It's not important.

Ann   It was two minutes ago. Lisa? Don't keep me in suspense.

Julie bursts in.

Julie   Lisa! I've got to tell... Mrs Jackson! I thought you'd be out.

Ann   Nice to see you too, pet.

Julie   I didn't mean it like that.

Lisa   Shut up, man. We've got some news. You're never going to believe this.

Julie   What?

Ann   Don't look so worried. You tell Julie. I'll see what old moany face has got to say about it. I'm just nipping up your nana's.

Julie   No!

Ann   You don't know what I'm going to tell her yet.

Julie   She was tired.

Lisa   Julie man, we're gonna meet Arthur Scargill! Me mam's going to be doing a speech on the same stage as Arthur.

Julie   Oh my God!

Lisa   In the new year.

Ann   I won't be long.

Ann exits.

Lisa   I've never seen me mam like this before, she's so happy.

Julie   So are you.

Lisa   Well, I've had a crap day and maybe this is a sign that things are going to get better. I think we should forget all about that night at the allotments.

Julie   So you're not gonna tell your mam about the affair?

Lisa   I can't now. You saw how happy she was. I'm sure it's all over by now. And our Maggie's definitely not pregnant, I'd be able to tell. We should forget it ever happened.

Julie   If you think it's best.

Lisa   We've got to. For everyone's sake. And what you don't know doesn't harm you.

SCENE TWELVE

The Christmas miracle

The Soup Kitchen, Christmas Day 1984, Band Aid's Do They Know It's Christmas? *is playing on the radio. Ann is wearing a well worn Christmas hat from of a cracker and Lisa has a home-made tinsel halo on her head.*

Ann   Don't throw those turkey scraps away, they'll do for the soup tomorrow.

Lisa   Julie's been ages up me nana's.

Ann   She's probably sitting with her while she has her dinner. You should have gone up.

Lisa   I was up this morning and I didn't see you there.

Ann   I was busy. I'm going later.

Lisa   Where's me dad?

Ann   Don't ask me, he was away straight after the

Christmas pudding. Probably up the allotments.

Lisa On Christmas day?

Ann Never mind him. Will you listen to me speech?

Lisa Have you finished it?

Ann Aye, Jude gave us a hand.

Lisa Mam, I'm so excited about going to London.

Ann Me too, but I won't be able to enjoy it, I'll be too nervous.

Lisa You'll be great, mam.

Ann Do you think?

Lisa Course you will, I'm dead proud of you.

Ann Are you pet?

Lisa Yes. We're gonna meet Arthur Scargill and it's all down to you. It's the best Christmas present ever.

Ann takes out her speech.

Ann Right, now you've got to be honest with me.

She starts reading.

Ann "My man's not perfect, I don't need anyone to tell me that."

Lisa Is it about me dad?

Ann Well I am a miner's wife. It's about all of us.

Give us a chance.

Ann   "But he's always been an honest man, a law-abiding, hard-working man, until nine months ago."

Julie bursts in wearing a halo just like Lisa's.

Julie   (*Breathless*) Maggie's had eight pups!

Ann   Pups!

Lisa   Yer jokin!

Julie   They're gorgeous. One's a bit small. We're not sure if he'll see the night out. But he's a fighter, like Arthur. He won't give up without a struggle. He's so cute.

Lisa   Eight pups!

Ann   How did she get pregnant?

Julie   I shouldn't think we need to draw you diagrams Mrs Jackson, not at your age.

Ann   I haven't given up the ghost yet.

Julie   (*Excited*) One minute she's not pregnant and the next minute she is, it's like... like a Christmas miracle.

Lisa   Calm down.

Julie   Maybe we should call one of them Jesus?

Ann   What's me mam said?

Julie   I think she's in shock. It's a good job Mr Jackson was there, he delivered them.

Ann   So that's where he's been.

Julie   He was like a proper vet. It was like *All Creatures Great and Small*, without the cows.

Lisa   (*To Julie*) Ha'way, let's go and see them.

Ann   You can't, we've got loads to do.

Julie   They're so cute.

Ann   They don't stay like that forever. How we gonna feed them?

Lisa   They drink milk for the first few weeks.

Ann   What then? We're skint.

Julie   Meatballs!

Ann   You can't feed dogs Russian meatballs!

Lisa   You feed us them.

Julie   They like them.

Ann   How do you know?

Lisa   She doesn't.

Julie   They're bound to.

Ann   They'll be too rich for their little stomachs and we cannot pinch from the kitchen.

Lisa   We'll think of something. Ha'way Julie. (*To Ann*) I won't be long.

Ann (*They leave*) But we've got all these dishes to do and you haven't heard me speech yet (*Shaking her head*) Bloody Maggie! How are we gonna manage?

SCENE THIRTEEN

Walking without the dog

The back field, a week later.

Julie It's weird walking without Maggie.

Lisa I know.

Julie She'll soon need walking, the pups are growing so fast. Should we go round and see them?

Lisa Best not, me nana's not well.

Julie She might need some help.

Lisa Me mam's with her.

Julie Have they made up?

Lisa They'd never really fallen out, they just didn't speak much. Me nana's over the moon that me mam's doing the speech. She said she wishes she could come to London to see her.

Julie It's freezin'.

Lisa Can we not go round yours?

Julie Naw, best not.

Lisa Ha'way man.

Julie   Me mam's in, she's getting right on me nerves. She keeps talking about the house being repossessed.

Lisa   Aye, well, everybody's in the same boat.

Julie   I know.

Lisa   Apart from the scabs. I don't know how they can live with themselves.

Julie   Yeah.

Lisa   My mam says she would rather eat grass than let me dad go back to work.

Julie   She's great, your mam.

Lisa   You wouldn't say that if she was practising her speech on yer every five minutes.

Julie   I can't believe we're going to see Arthur this Thursday!

Lisa   I know, it's great. Is your mam letting you bunk off for the rally?

Julie   I haven't asked her yet, the mood she's in.

Lisa   Well she'd better say yes, cos I'm not going without you.

Julie   You don't know what she's like.

Lisa   Don't ask her then, just say that you're staying at mine.

Julie   For two nights?

Lisa   Just ask for one. As long as we get to London, we can worry about what you tell her on the way back. Ha'way man Julie, where's your bottle?

Julie   Aye, you're right.

Lisa   Of course I am. And besides, I've arranged to go round nana's tomorrow to finish off our jeans. She says we can use her bath to bleach them.

Julie   We're gonna look great walking past Buckingham Palace with our bleached jeans and our 'coal not dole' T-shirts.

Lisa   The march isn't going past Buckingham Palace.

Julie   Well, Big Ben then.

Lisa   We'll look great. Are you wearing your Docs?

Julie   Aye, me feet were killin' after the gala in your court shoes. (*Pause*) Lisa, I've got a confession to make.

Lisa   What?

Julie   You're me best friend, aren't you?

Lisa   Course I'm your best friend.

Julie   Promise you won't go off it.

Lisa   Cross me heart and hope to die. What is it? (*Julie doesn't answer*) Julie, you're scaring us, what is it?

Julie   I've broken the heel on your court shoe.

Lisa   You daft bugger, I thought it was something serious.

Julie   It is, they're patent leather.

Lisa   Julie, you're the best friend in the whole world. It doesn't matter what you've broken.

Julie   I thought you'd go mad.

Lisa   Don't be daft.

Julie   Together forever?

Lisa   Together forever.

SCENE FOURTEEN

Fading Light

Dot's living room the next day. It is evening. Dot is collapsed in the armchair, she appears to be sleeping. Outside we hear police sirens and miners chanting "Scab scab! scab!" And then singing:

I'd rather be a picket than a scab
I'd rather be a picket than a scab
I'd rather be a picket
Rather be a picket
Rather be a picket than a scab

Lisa and Julie enter.

Julie   There's a right commotion going on out there. I've never seen so many coppers.

Lisa   They must be bussing the scabs in. (*Lisa looks out of the window*)

Julie   Yer alright, Mrs Stavers?

Lisa   Nana, have you got that bleach?

Julie   I think she's asleep.

Lisa   Nana?

Lisa approaches her, Dot vomits.

Lisa   Oh my God, she must be having one of her funny turns.

Julie   *Urrgh*!

Lisa   Julie, man, get some water or something.

Julie   What's wrong?

Lisa   She's really not well.

Julie   Are you alright, Mrs Stavers? I think we should phone for an ambulance.

Lisa   She hasn't got a phone, man.

Julie   Oh God. How long do you think she's been like that?

Lisa   I dunno.

Julie   You'll be fine, Mrs Stavers. Just breathe deeply, don't panic.

Lisa   I feel sick.

Julie   I thought you wanted to be a midwife! Run to the phone and call for an ambulance.

Dot   Ann, I want my Ann.

Julie   See if you can fetch your mam, while you're at it.

Dot   I don't want to go, I'm not ready.

Julie   Now!

Lisa exits.

Julie   You're going nowhere, do you hear? I'm not gonna let you. You're staying here with me. Right? Until Lisa gets back, she's gone to fetch help.

Dot   Has she gone to fetch our Ann?

Lisa   Yes, they'll be back soon. I'm gonna get you some water. Don't you go anywhere, mind. I'll just be a minute.

Julie exits to the kitchen. Dot lurches weakly in and out of consciousness.

Dot   Julie, I need to speak to you.

Julie   (*From in the kitchen*) I'm coming.

Julie enters with a glass of water and a wet cloth.

Dot   I need to ask you...

Julie   Have a drink first.

Dot   I can't.

Julie   Just a little one, there, that's better.

Dot   What did you hear? (*Julie doesn't respond*) We haven't got long.

Julie   I heard it all. About the affair and that stupid card. I haven't told anyone, not even Lisa.

Dot   Good lass.

Julie   (*Mopping her brow*) There, this will cool you down. Is that better?

Dot   You've got to destroy that card. Promise.

Julie   I promise.

Dot   I feel crap pet, I think this is it.

Julie   You've got to hang on, stay awake.

Dot   I don't want to go, Julie. Don't let me die.

Julie   I won't. You'll be alright, I promise.

Dot   Promises, promises.

Julie mops her brow. Lisa bursts in. We hear an aggravated crowd chanting, "Scab! scab! scab! scab!"

Julie   Jesus, where have you been?

Lisa   The doctor will be here soon.

Julie   The doctor? What happened to the fuckin' ambulance?

Lisa   (*Whispering*) Shush! You'll get her even more worked up. There's loads of trouble, the police are everywhere.

Julie   Is your mam coming?

Lisa   There was no one in.

Julie   You should have went up the kitchen.

Lisa   I tried, but I couldn't get through – the police wouldn't let us. I saw me dad, he said they've sealed the village off, no one gets in or out, even ambulances. That's why he's ran up for the doctor.

Julie   Well he'd better hurry up. Mrs Stavers, Mrs Stavers.

Julie slaps her cheek.

Lisa   Nana? Wake up. Wake up! Do something, Julie.

Julie   I'm trying. Lisa, give her the kiss of life.

Lisa   I can't.

Julie   You've got to.

Lisa   Get her onto the floor.

They put her in the recovery position. Lisa goes to remove Dot's false teeth.

Julie   (*Repulsed*) What you doing?

Lisa   You've got to take their teeth out, in case they choke.

Julie   She looks weird.

Lisa   Shut up, Julie.

They pause and look at Dot's body.

Julie   She's dead, isn't she?

Lisa   No she's not, she can't be. (*Sobbing*) She can't be.

Julie   Leave her, Lisa. She's gone.

SCENE FIFTEEN

Life, death and Brian Clough

Dot's back yard. Later the same night. Blue flashing light fades as the ambulance drives away. The girls are sitting on Dot's step, staring ahead, not talking. Ray approaches them.

Ray   Yer alright?

They look at him.

Ray   I know, daft question. (*Long pause*) You did a grand job back there.

Lisa   Dad, she's dead.

Ray   I know pet, it's crap. But yous did everything you could. Sometimes that's all you can do.

Julie   Maybe if we'd done something different.

Ray   Don't blame yourselves, it's not your fault.

Lisa   No, it's the police's fault. If the ambulance could've got through...

Ray   If ifs and ands were pots and pans...

Julie   (*Joining in*) There'd be no need for tinkers.

Lisa   What does that mean?

Ray   It's happened Lise, we can't change it. As much as we want to, we can't.

Lisa   Why though? Why now?

Ray   I don't know, pet. I wish I could give you all the right answers, but sometimes life's, well, it's just a bit of a bastard, and there's no explanations. One day everything's fine and then in one second it can all be over. (*Pause*) It's like football. (*The girls raise their eyes, they've heard the football analogies before*) Hear us out, lasses. Brian Clough, one day he was scoring goals like there was no tomorrow, bad choice of words. He was our top goal scorer and this one day he pulls his boots on for a match, against Bury, not realising that it was going to be his last, bloody Boxing Day and all, fine Christmas present that was.

Julie   Did he die?

Ray   No. He went in for this ball up against the keeper, and bang, his knee's gone, career was over.

Lisa   That's nowt like what happened to me nana.

Ray   No, course not. Brian Clough went on to have a successful managerial career. But what I'm trying to say is that life can change just like that. It can be so fragile, it hangs on a... it's balanced on something as... (*He motions something tiny with his fingers*) as small as a gnat's bollock.

Lisa and Julie can't quite believe what they've just heard. Lisa storms off in a huff.

Ray   I'm not helping matters, am I? Where's Ann when you need her? I can't believe she's off to Newcastle for a bloody rally, tonight of all nights.

Julie   I'm glad you're here, Mr Jackson.

Ray   Are you?

Julie   Yes.

Ray   After what I've done?

Julie   Ann will be really upset when you tell her.

Ray   What do you mean?

Julie   About her mam.

Ray   Ah, right. Yes, she'll be gutted. It took her ages to get over her dad's death, she was really close to him.

Julie   Like you and Lisa.

Ray   She means everything to me.

A dog barks.

Julie   Oh my god. What's going to happen to Maggie and the pups?

Ray   Bloody hell, I'd forgotten all about them little buggers.

Julie   They'll have to go and live with you.

Ray   That should cheer our Lisa up a bit.

SCENE SIXTEEN

Heaven Knows I'm Miserable Now

Lisa's bedroom the next day. Lisa and Julie are flicking through magazines, disinterested.

Lisa   I can't get excited about Thursday. I mean, I want to see Arthur, but I keep thinking about me nana.

Julie   I know. But you've got to stay strong, for the sake of the puppies.

Lisa   Me mam's really worried because they haven't got any money to pay for puppies, never mind the funeral. I think they'll sell them.

Julie   We're gonna meet Arthur anyway, we don't need the money.

Lisa   (*Thinking*) Did me nana say anything before she died?

Julie   What like?

Lisa   I dunno. It'd be nice to know what her last words were. I was really off with her a few months ago. I wouldn't listen and now I feel really bad. It was as if she was trying to tell me something.

Julie   You can't think like that, Lisa. She loved you, that's all you need to know.

Lisa   Do you think she can see us?

Julie   I bet she can. And do you know, she'd be mad at us for moping around.

Lisa   You're right. She'd want us to be excited about going to see Arthur.

Julie   Did you see him on the news at dinner time?

Lisa   No.

Julie   They make out that he's a right trouble maker.

Lisa   I know. And he's only sticking up for us.

Julie   He's really clever, isn't he?

Lisa   Yeah, he's dead honest. He's the only one telling the truth about what's going on.

Julie   He looks a bit like me uncle.

Lisa   (*Incredulous*) Yer uncle? (*Laughs*)

Julie   Yeah.

Lisa   You fancy someone who looks like your uncle?

Julie   You fancy him, I don't really fancy him.

Lisa   I don't fancy him, I just think he's clever.

Julie   Yeah, so do I.

Lisa   Yeah, but you think he looks like your uncle.

Lisa bursts out laughing, they play-fight.

Julie   Lisa!

Lisa   (*Mimicking*) "Yes, Mr and Mrs Jackson, I fancy me boyfriend who looks like me uncle."

Julie   He's not my boyfriend! He's your boyfriend.

Lisa   Yeah, right!

Julie   Yeah, right. I think I like George Michael better.

Lisa is shocked.

Lisa   Julie!

Julie   Only jokin'! Like I'd fancy that hairy poser.

They laugh.

Julie   The rally's gonna be great, isn't it.

Lisa   Yeah. We'll have a right laugh, for nana.

Ann knocks and enters. She is very subdued.

Lisa   We've just been talking about the rally.

Julie   I can't wait to hear your speech.

Lisa   You're not gonna practise it again, are you?

Ann   No, love.

Julie   Shut up, man, she's nervous.

Ann   I've just had Marjorie at the door.

Lisa   The vicar's wife?

Ann   They've set a date for the funeral. It's this Thursday.

The girls are speechless.

Ann   Lisa I... I know how much...

Lisa   It's alright. We can't miss me nana's funeral.

Ann   I'm really sorry.

Lisa   What about Julie?

Ann   (*To Julie*) It's up to you love, you've got to decide. But you'd be very welcome at the funeral.

Julie   I'd like to come, Mrs Jackson.

Long pause.

Lisa   It's alright, mam, it's not your fault.

Ann   I really wanted to give that speech. It was my chance to show everyone what I could do. Me mam, Ray...

Lisa   You don't have to prove yourself to us, mam.

Julie   I think you're great, Mrs Jackson.

Lisa   Thanks, Julie, love. You've been great. I'm so glad Lisa's got a friend like you.

Julie   We'll be friends forever, Mrs Jackson.

Ann   I'm sure you will. You two just stick together, because life can be so cruel.

Julie   It's like Brian Clough, Mrs Jackson.

Ann   Brian Clough? What's he got to...

Lisa   (*Interrupting*) Nothing. We'll be alright, mam. We've got each other.

Ann   I'm gonna (*She indicates that she is leaving*) put the kettle on.

Ann exits, leaving the girls sitting staring forlornly.

SCENE SEVENTEEN

The wake

Lisa and Julie are outside The Jacksons' house dressed in black. The wake is happening inside. They are eating crisps out of bowls.

Julie   What the vicar said was lovely.

Lisa   Do you want some more cheese 'n' onion?

Julie   No, just stay out here – I don't want to go back inside. Everyone's drunk and crying, even Davy Turner. He's had too much home brew.

Lisa   He deserves it. He had a whip round to help pay for the funeral and got onto the union. They put the rest in.

Julie   That was nice.

Lisa   I wish me mam hadn't took us to see her.

Julie   What's the chapel of rest like?

Lisa   Horrible. It smells funny. Me mam said it was the preservatives.

Julie   Preservatives?

Lisa   They preserve them, before they put them in the coffin.

Julie   Was she in a coffin?

Lisa   What do you think she was in?

Julie   I dunno, I thought she'd be like on a bed, surrounded by roses.

Lisa   It's not sleeping beauty.

Julie   I wouldn't have fancied seeing her in a coffin. It was bad enough seeing it in the church today.

Lisa   She was a proper corpse, she was grey and bony. All her features were pointy.

Julie   Don't upset yourself.

Lisa   I suppose this is as bad as it gets, me nana's dead and we're not even going to meet Arthur. At least we've still got the puppies.

Julie   (*Thinking*) If you don't have to sell the pups to pay for the funeral, we can still sell them and use the money to meet Arthur. Then 'Operation Ginger Comby-over' wasn't such a bad idea after all. Maybes it was meant to be.

Lisa   Do you reckon?

Julie   Could be. Maybe your nana is watching over us.

Ray enters, slightly drunk and troubled.

Ray   Lisa, get in the house.

Julie and Lisa think Ray is kidding.

Ray   Get in the house.

Lisa   Dad, it's depressing in there.

Ray   I won't tell you again.

Lisa   Alright keep your hair on, we're going.

Ray   Not you Julie.

Lisa   What's going on?

Ray   In. Now.

Lisa   I haven't even done owt.

Lisa goes inside.

Julie   Mr Jackson?

Ray   You'd better be away home.

Julie   I didn't know... It's Maggie's fault.

Ray   You knew.

Julie   It was a mistake.

Ray   It was that alright.

Julie   Honest, we didn't know she have all those pups, it got out of hand.

Ray   Eh? What yer on about?

Julie   (*Back-pedalling*) Nothing. I want to see Lisa.

Ray   Listen, Julie, I think it's probably a good idea if you don't see Lisa for a while.

Julie   She's me best friend, I've got to see her. She's upset about her nana.

Ray   Julie, go home.

Julie   But Mr...

Ray   Just bugger off, will you. I don't want to see you round here again.

Ray walks off, upset. Julie is left standing with tears in her eyes.

Julie   But I haven't done anything.

SCENE EIGHTEEN

Whose Side Are You On?

Lisa's bedroom. Lights up on Lisa being hugged by Ann. Lisa is crying, Ann is on the verge of tears.

Lisa   Will you get rid of everyone downstairs.

Ann   I cannot just chuck them out, it's your nana's wake.

Lisa   Do they all know?

Ann   Everyone in the colliery knows, pet. It's written on the Co-op wall.

Lisa   You've got to tell them all that it's not her fault. You've got to explain to me dad.

Ann   I know, pet, but its not as simple as that.

Lisa   You're on his side?

Ann   He is me husband, Lisa.

Lisa   And I'm your daughter! And Julie's me best friend, and it's not fair.

Ann   Julie's dad knew what would happen if he went back. He's scabbed. He's betrayed us, Lisa, and he's betrayed his daughter.

Lisa   She doesn't even like him.

Ann   She's his flesh and blood, he's her dad. She's only young, she'll be on his side.

Lisa   Will you stop going on about sides. It's not a war, it's a strike.

Ann   It is a war. I wish I could tell you different pet, but I can't and if we lose it, we're finished.

Lisa   Is that what Jude told you?

Ann   I've got me own opinions, you know. I don't need anybody else to tell me what to think.

Lisa   Then why are you doing it to me?

Ann   I'm not trying to tell you what to think. But this is bigger than us. It's bigger than just you and Julie. If the pit goes, god only knows what will happen, it'll be like a ghost town. You've just got to look at other villages where pits have closed. We're fighting, me and your dad, and all the others out on strike, we're fighting for your future. Julie's dad has betrayed us for a few quid. He's gone to fight for the other side and there's no coming back. Remember what you told me Arthur had said at the gala, about sticking together or we'll lose? Well this is what he meant. (*Long pause, Ann strokes Lisa's hair*) People can be cruel, Lisa. It might get nasty and me and your dad don't want you involved, we don't want you to get hurt.

Lisa   I already am.

SCENE NINETEEN

Shoes and wash day blues

The Jacksons' back yard, a few days later. Ann is pegging out the washing. Julie appears over the wall, she is wearing new glasses.

Julie   If the path's dry, it'll dry.

Ann   Julie?

Julie   Don't look at us like that, Mrs Jackson.

Ann   You shouldn't be here, Julie.

Julie   I had to. (*She hands over a carrier bag*) Lisa's shoes, I've had them for ages. I thought I better bring them back. They're her favourites, they go with her leggings.

Ann   The heel's off.

Julie   I tried to fix it.

Ann   You'll be able to afford a new pair soon. Just like yer new glasses.

Julie   I prefer me old ones.

Ann   Yer going to have to go.

Julie   Tell Lisa I'm sorry.

Ann   So are we, Julie, so are we.

Julie   I'm sorry, Mrs Jackson. For coming round. I thought she might need her shoes for school. They're her only black ones. If she wants to borrow some of mine...

Ann   Go away, Julie. We don't need charity from a... (*She breaks off*)

Julie   From a scab? Go on, you might as well say it, cos you're treating us like one, just like everyone else around here. I thought you were different, I loved you more than I loved me own family.

Julie exits crying. Lisa enters.

Lisa   Has she gone?

Ann   Yes.

Lisa (*Shouting over the wall*) Scab! Piss off you bloody scabby bastard! (*To Ann*) Are you happy now?

SCENE TWENTY

You've Got Everything Now

Immediately after, in the back lane. Julie is running away, upset. She sees Ray walking towards her. They stop in their tracks.

Julie Before you say anything, I'm going. OK? And if you want to call us a scab, say it to me face. I couldn't feel any worse than I do already do.

Ray Don't do this, Julie.

Julie Don't look down your nose at me!

Ray Go home, pet.

Julie You're not so great yourself, you know? Everyone thinks you're the perfect little family, but I know better.

Ray Julie, you're upset. Just go home.

Julie Will you stop tellin' me to go home, I don't want to go home. Look at you, you think you're Mr Wonderful and we all know you're having it off with the copper's wife.

Ray What did you say?

Julie You heard.

Ray You're talkin' rubbish. You've got the wrong end of the stick.

Julie I heard everything, *Ray*. I heard the whole lot, that day when I came back from the post office.

Ray   You sly little...

Julie   Sly? Me? Look in the mirror! I've been keeping your little secret longer than you think. We know what you are. We know. We know you're nowt but a hypocrite. We heard you, man! We were up the allotments, that night with the dogs.

Ray   Who's we?

Julie   Are you frightened your precious little daughter knows?

Ray   Who else knows? You and our Lisa?

Julie   Yes, me and daddy's girl, she knows what you're like. You treat me like I'm the scab, like I'm a traitor, and I've done nothing wrong! But you! All along you were having it off with the copper's wife.

Ray   Keep your voice down.

Julie   (*She laughs*) Why should I? I've got nowt to lose. But you... (*Ray exits quickly, walking back in the direction he came from as Julie's laughter turns to tears*) you've still got everything.

SCENE TWENTY ONE

Daddy's girl grows up

The next day, Lisa's bedroom. Lisa is finishing off a letter.

Lisa   Love, Lisa (*Sighing, she writes three kisses, putting the card in an envelope. Ray enters. Lisa hides the letter.*)

Ray   (*Awkwardly*) Did your mam tell you about her speech at the Yorkshire rally.

Lisa   (*Uninterested*) Yeah.

Ray   You'll get to see Arthur.

Lisa   It's Julie I want to see.

Ray   What you hiding?

Lisa   It's private.

Ray   You're keeping a lot to yourself. You never talk to me these days. We used to have a laugh and a joke.

Lisa   I don't feel like laughing.

Ray   You've had a tough time of it.

Lisa   Why did the chicken cross the road twice?

Ray   Lisa, you don't have to.

Lisa   Because it was a double-crosser.

Long pause. Ray breathes deeply.

Ray   I know, you know.

Lisa   Know what?

Ray   Know about, well, what you're not supposed to know about.

Lisa   No, dad, I don't know.

Ray   About the allotments, that night with the dogs. Julie told me you were there.

Lisa   She had no business. When did you see her?

Ray   Yesterday. (*Long pause*) Why didn't you tell your mam?

Lisa   (*Shrugs*) I was going to.

Ray   I'm sorry, Lisa.

Lisa   Are you still seeing her? (*Ray looks away*) You are, aren't you?

Ray   No! Well...

Lisa   Don't lie to us.

Ray   I'll finish it. Now. That's it, it's over.

Lisa   Just like that? Do you not love her?

Ray   She means nothing.

Lisa   How can you say that? You've cheated on me mam. And she means nothing to you?

Ray   This isn't Mills and Boon, Lisa; it isn't all hearts and bloody flowers. You're fifteen, you know nowt about real life.

Lisa   Real life? Don't you mean sex? I do know. I know that me dad's a liar and hypocrite, and me mam deserves better. She's doing everything to support you. She's even getting up on stage, in front of thousands of people. She's terrified, for you.

Ray   It's not for me.

Lisa   Course it is. Have you not heard her speech? No. Because you're too busy having it away with the copper's missus to support your own wife. You're a fool. It's all about you.

Ray   I'm sorry.

Lisa   She deserves something better.

Ray   You're right, I've been stupid. I am a fool. This'll never happen again. I'm gonna come clean, I'm gonna tell your mam everything. We'll start over with a clean slate.

Lisa   Self, self, self.

Ray   I thought that's what you wanted.

Lisa   To make you feel better? To ease your guilty conscience. No, that's not what I want.

Ray   Well, what?

Lisa   Look at you.

Ray   I love her. I love you.

Lisa   Then why did you do it? If she finds out that you've been messing around with a copper's wife, it'll be over.

Ray   What am I gonna do?

Lisa   Nothing. You tell her nothing. (*To herself*) Me nana tried to tell us. (*Forcefully, to Ray*) Remember *Casablanca*? "The problems of three little people don't amount to a hill of beans in this crazy world." (*To herself*) This is what she meant. (*To Ray*) *They* were fighting Hitler and *we* are fighting Thatcher, and we've got to win. We've got to put our own feelings aside and look at the big picture.

Ray   It would destroy her if she found out.

Lisa   No dad, it wouldn't. She's strong, but she needs all her energy for the big fight, she needs to be part of it, and she needs to do that speech.

Ray   I feel terrible.

Lisa   So you should, and you're gonna feel worse, everyday that you have to carry this secret. Knowing that I know. It'll burn away inside you, like it did with me. This is your punishment.

Ray   I'm sorry.

Lisa   Not as sorry as I am.

Ray   You seem to have grown up all of a sudden. You don't need me anymore, but I still need you, Lisa. You'll always be my little girl. (*Long pause*) I'll deliver that letter for you. (*She looks at him, guarded*) You've got to trust me, Lisa.

Lisa thinks about it. She hands over the letter. Ray exits.

SCENE TWENTY TWO

Beyond the grave

The Jacksons' living room. Ann is looking through some photos of her mother. She has been crying.

Ann   You're going to have to help me get through this, mam. I'm going to do this speech and you're going to have to help me. "My man's not perfect, I don't need anyone to tell me that. But he's always been a good man, an honest man, a hardworking man. Until nine months ago. This strike has changed people, it's changed me. A lot has happened to test us. My mother died, we didn't even have the money to bury her..." (*She breaks down in tears*) Oh Mam, I'm sorry, I'm sorry I blamed you for everything. But you broke me dad's heart. I always took his side, like our Lisa does with Ray. She's growing up so quickly, she's just like you, headstrong, opinionated. I just hope we're doing the right thing by her, what with all this business with Julie. I know I didn't do the right thing with you, I should have been a better daughter. I'm sorry. I'm sorry I didn't spend more time with you. I'm so (*sobbing*) sorry.

SCENE TWENTY THREE

Back To The Old House

Dot's living room. Julie is searching through Dot's handbag. She finds the card. Lisa enters, Julie puts the card in her pocket.

Lisa   Lost something?

They stare at each other, clearly glad to see each other, but a bit awkward.

Julie   I thought I had.

They embrace.

Lisa   I'm glad you're here.

Julie   Me too.

Lisa   I didn't know if you'd get the note.

Julie   Me mam nearly saw it. I thought you hated me, until I got that letter.

Lisa   I don't hate you. It's not your fault your dad's a scab. (*Julie shoots her a hurt glance*) Sorry. (*Pause*) Arthur's going to be at a rally in Yorkshire next month.

Julie   Is he?

Lisa We could go together.

Julie They'd never let me on the coach.

Lisa We could make our own way there.

Julie Just the two of us?

Lisa Yeah, why not? If we want to be friends, it's got nothing to do with anyone else.

Julie Yes it has. I get called a scab everywhere I go. Even that little scruff Jimmy Morgan spat in me face.

Lisa I'll kill him.

Julie No you won't. It's not just about us. It's about everyone else sticking their oar in. How can we see each other now?

Lisa It's like *Casablanca*.

Julie Can I be Ingrid Bergman?

Lisa What will I do without you?

Julie Maybe we could still meet up in secret.

Lisa Yes. At the allotments.

Julie What about your dad?

Lisa He wouldn't say anything, not now.

Julie I thought he hated me.

Lisa He delivered the letter.

Julie Your dad?

Lisa   Yes, me dad. Why did you tell him we knew? It was our secret.

Julie   I was upset.

Lisa   It's probably for the best.

Julie   Do you think?

Lisa   It's all over now.

Julie   What did he say?

Lisa   He's gonna pack her in.

Julie   Does your mam know?

Lisa   No. We've got to keep this quiet, she must never find out, ever. But this is the last, no more secrets after this. Promise me that we'll never be like them, keeping things back.

Julie   (*Light-heartedly*) What you don't know doesn't harm you.

Lisa   Julie, I mean it.

Julie   No more secrets.

Lisa   Ever.

Julie takes out the card and hands it to Lisa.

Julie   Your nana knew.

Lisa   Nana? (*Referring to the card*) This is disgusting.

Julie   She'd found it in your dad's pocket, when she was doing the washing.

Lisa   How do you know?

Julie   The day I went for your nana's money, I walked in
on her and your dad arguing.

Lisa   She knew and she didn't say anything?

Julie   Neither did we. She didn't want to hurt you or your
mam. (*Pause*) There's more... (*Pause*) the reason your mam and
your nana didn't get on was because your nana had an affair.

Lisa   (*Incredulous*) Me nana? God, everybody's at it!

Julie   It was years ago.

Lisa   You knew all this and you didn't tell me.

Julie   I tried, that night I came round to tell you. But you
told me about Arthur and you seemed so happy. I hadn't seen
you that happy in ages.

Lisa   The lies go on and on.

Julie   We can end them. Like you want. Like your nana
wanted. The night she died, she made me promise to destroy
the card. That was her final wish. Let's do it together, let's end
this whole thing now.

Lisa   (*Long pause*) There's some matches in the kitchen.

*Julie exits and returns with a metal bucket and matches. She sets the bucket
down.*

Julie   Ready?

Lisa holds the card over the bucket.

Julie   For the future.

Lisa   For me mam, for me dad, for me nana.

Julie strikes the match.

Julie   For us.

The card catches light and they drop it into the bucket.

SCENE TWENTY FOUR

Words of support

Ray is reading Ann's speech. He has tears in his eyes. Ann is watching.

Ann   It's not that bad, is it?

Ray   It's great. Really great.

Ann   Because it's about you?

Ray   Don't be daft.

Ann   It was supposed to be a big secret.

Ray   I never liked secrets.

Ann   I'm terrified, Ray. What if I freeze on stage in front of all those people? I'd be mortified. Our Lisa would never speak to us.

Ray   You're not gonna freeze. You're not gonna let anyone down. Especially our Lisa.

Ann   I might forget me lines.

Ray   Then speak from the heart. You tell them what's in here. (*Holds his fist against his chest*) That's all that counts.

Ann   And what's up here. (*Points to her head*)

Ray   This is the last push, Ann. We can get through this. I'll be there with our Lisa and all the lasses from the kitchen, we'll be rooting for you. You'll be great. I promise.

Ann   But will we win?

Ray   I don't know, but we can't give up. Not now.

Ann   Not ever.

SCENE TWENTY FIVE

Say Hello, Wave Goodbye

Lisa, Ann and Ray are standing at the bus stop. Ann has a clipboard. Lisa wears her 'coal not dole' T-shirt.

Lisa   I've been waiting for this day for ages. I'm going to meet Arthur Scargill and I'm not even excited.

Ann   You've grown up so much, pet.

Ray   We've all changed.

Lisa   I'm dead proud of you mam. I can't wait to hear your speech.

Ray   You can say that again.

Ann   (*To Lisa*) Thanks love. (*She smiles at Ray*)

Lisa   Me nana would have loved this.

Ann   She's here. (*Ann presses her hand on her heart*)

Lisa   But Julie isn't.

Ann   No, pet.

Ray   Here's the buses.

Ann   I'd better round everyone up.

Ann exits.

Ray   At least one of you will get to meet Arthur.

Lisa   It's not fair, dad. (*Half laughing*) And don't you dare mention Brian Clough.

Ray   Come here.

Ray hugs her to him, they start to walk off. Julie enters.

Julie   Lisa, wait.

Lisa   What are you doing here?

Julie   Hello, Mr Jackson.

Ray   I'll leave you to it. (*To Lisa*) Don't be long.

Julie   I had to come.

Lisa   But the coaches are full, you can't come.

Julie   I'm not coming with you. I've come to say goodbye, we're leaving the village.

Lisa   You can't.

Julie   Me mam's had enough.

Lisa   Where you going?

Julie   Sunderland. To me nana's.

Lisa   You can't just move.

Julie   Me dad was beaten up last night. He had to go to hospital.

Lisa   Is he OK?

Julie   The cuts and bruises'll heal.

Lisa   Oh Julie. What am I gonna do?

Julie   You'll look after those puppies.

Lisa   You can't just leave.

Julie   It's getting dangerous. Arthur said it was just a matter of sticking together. (*Light-heartedly*) Arthur bloody Scargill, what does he know?

Lisa   It isn't his fault.

Julie   Well whose is it? It's not mine.

Lisa   Arthur was right, he didn't let us down. Everyone else did.

Julie   It still feels the same from where I'm standing. Together forever. (*Half-laughs*)

Lisa   I meant every word of it.

Julie   But it's bigger than just us.

Lisa   It shouldn't have to be.

Julie   No. But it is. I'll miss you.

Lisa   You're the best friend, ever.

Julie   They're all waiting for you. Don't miss your bus.

Lisa exits, leaving Julie standing.

THE END

New Writing North

New Writing North is the writing development agency for the north east of England. We aim to create an environment in the region in which new writing in all genres can flourish and develop. We are a unique organisation within the UK, merging as we do individual development work with writers across all media with educational work and the production of creative projects. We work with writers from different genres and forms to develop career opportunities, new commissions, projects, residencies, publications and live events.

We work in partnership with a broad range of organisations, universities, local authorities, regional development agencies, sponsors and media producers to develop opportunities for writers in our region.

We manage the *Northern Writers' Awards* and the *Northern Rock Foundation Writer's Award* (currently the largest literary award in the UK and worth £60,000 to the winning writer) and support writers at all stages of their careers by career mentoring and by the creation of professional development training initiatives and projects.

We work in partnership with writers, theatres and producers to develop new writing for the stage and have initiated work and new commissions with many of the theatre companies in our region. We also produce new plays as part of a regional touring consortium.

Though our international work we aspire to create partnerships and projects for writers from our region with their international counterparts. We are currently developing projects in Bulgaria, Siberia and the Czech Republic.

We run a wide-ranging education and community programme which involves the development of creative projects with writers and young people both inside and outside of schools.

We are working with Orange to develop activities for young writers aged 11-18 to help develop the next generation of creative writers in our region. The Orange Young Writer's Festival runs across the

North East every summer and is supported by
www.wordmavericks.com

Published work includes *Bound*, a collection of short stories inspired
by County Durham, and *Kaput!* by Margaret Wilkinson.
Forthcoming published work includes *Writer-to-Writer*, new short
stories emerging from the *Festival of Stories*; *Magnetic North*, a collection
of work from North East writers which has been commissioned for
live performance; and *Eating the Elephant and Other Plays* by Julia
Darling.

Claire Malcolm
Director
claire@newwritingnorth.com

Anna Summerford
Education director
anna@newwritingnorth.com

For more information on our work

New Writing North
2 School Lane
Whickham
Newcastle upon Tyne
NE16 4SL
E: mail@newwritingnorth.com
T: 0191 488 8580

www.newwritingnorth.com
www.literaturenortheast.co.uk
www.nr-foundationwriters.com